STATE OF AFFAIRS:
NATIVE AMERICANS
IN THE 21ST CENTURY

NATIVE AMERICAN INDUSTRY
IN CONTEMPORARY AMERICA

TAMMY GAGNE

Mitchell Lane
PUBLISHERS
P.O. Box 196
Hockessin, Delaware 19707
Visit us on the web: www.mitchelllane.com
Comments? Email us: mitchelllane@mitchelllane.com

STATE OF AFFAIRS:
NATIVE AMERICANS
IN THE 21ST CENTURY

Preserving Their Heritage
Native Americans and the Government
Native American Industry in Contemporary America
Life on the Reservations

PUBLISHER'S NOTE: The facts on which the story
in this book is based have been thoroughly
researched. Documentation of such research
can be found on page 45. While every possible
effort has been made to ensure accuracy, the
publisher will not assume liability for damages
caused by inaccuracies in the data, and
makes no warranty on the accuracy of the
information contained herein.

ABOUT THE AUTHOR:
Tammy Gagne has written numerous books for
adults and children, including *A Kid's Guide
to the Voting Process* and *The Power of the
States* for Mitchell Lane Publishers. She counts
American history and civics among her many
interests. She resides in northern New England
with her husband and son. One of her favorite
pastimes is visiting schools to speak to kids
about the writing process.

Printing 1 2 3 4 5 6 7 8 9

**Library of Congress
Cataloging-in-Publication Data**
Gagne, Tammy.
 Native American industry in contemporary
America / by Tammy Gagne.
    pages cm.—(State of affairs: Native
Americans in the 21st century)
 Includes bibliographical references and index.
 ISBN 978-1-61228-443-9 (library bound)
 1. Indian business enterprises--United States-
-Juvenile literature. 2. Indians of North
America—Gaming—Juvenile literature.
 3. Indians of North America—Economic
conditions—Juvenile literature. I. Title.
 E98.B87G35 2014
 338.9730089'97—dc23
                                            2013017855

eBook ISBN: 9781612285047

PLB

CONTENTS

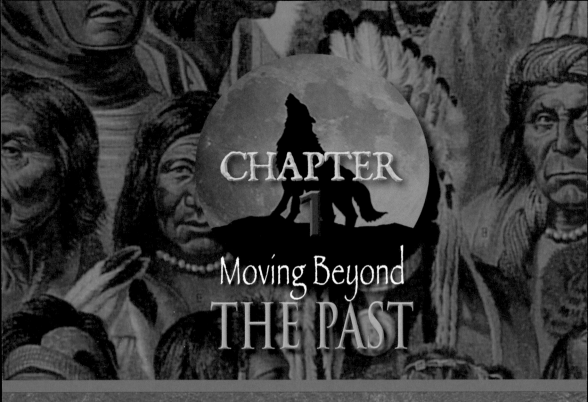

CHAPTER 1

Moving Beyond THE PAST

And the winner is . . . Cherokee Data Solutions. It might not be the first type of company that springs to mind when one thinks about Native American business, but perhaps it should be. This small technology company in Claremore, Oklahoma, and its founder, Pamela Huddleston Bickford, are proving to be a big inspiration for other companies in Native American industry. Cherokee Data Solutions was named the 2010 National Supplier of the Year by the National Minority Supplier Development Council. The same year, Bickford was chosen as the 2010 Oklahoma 8(a) Minority Small Business Person of the Year by the US Small Business Administration.

Bickford started Cherokee Data Solutions shortly after coming back to Oklahoma in 1999. She and her husband had moved their family to Texas when he was transferred with his job. She recalls, "That's when I thought, 'Never again.' We're not going to be at the beck and call of the economy and anything else that comes to make us move away from our family and our tribe."[1]

Pamela Huddleston Bickford is the founder of Cherokee Data Solutions. The company provides computer accessories, printer supplies, and data storage products to nearly every US state. In all it provides more than 700,000 different products to more than 400 businesses. Through CDS, Bickford has created numerous jobs for Native Americans in rural Oklahoma.

Bickford isn't alone in her efforts to grow Cherokee Data Solutions. She has six full-time employees and fourteen subcontractors. Together they serve more than 400 business customers in the government, tribal, education, and commercial sectors. "The opportunity to build and grow and create jobs is incredible, and with that comes an incredible amount of stress." Bickford admits. "I didn't expect that pressure when I started the company. On one side it's scary, and on the other side it's really cool. It's cool to see the employees going back to school or getting unique certifications . . . and overcoming personal challenges and stretching themselves, seeing them grow."[2]

The livelihoods of Native American people have changed a lot in the last several hundred years. At one time, most members of Indian tribes put food on their tables by hunting and farming. But eventually, the United States and its citizens began to

The lives of Native Americans changed dramatically in the years following the white settlers' arrival. Activities like buffalo hunting were soon replaced with European methods of providing for their families, like farming. The Cherokee tried to adopt many of the white settlers' ways, but what most of the whites really wanted was for Native people to leave the area.

challenge the Native people for their land and other resources. By the early 1800s, white Americans were moving into the southeastern United States, and they wanted land to grow their own crops. They knew that the soil in the South was ideal for growing cotton. White Americans also soon discovered large amounts of gold in Georgia. The only thing that stood between them and these valuable resources were the Native American tribes that were already there.

The Native people tried to defend their homes. Most of the battles ended in devastating losses for tribes in Alabama, Georgia, and Tennessee. A few tribes continued to fight, but they stood little chance against the US government and its army. In 1830, President Andrew Jackson passed the Indian Removal Act. This law offered two options to Native Americans living in the South: stay and become citizens of the United States or move west of the Mississippi River. The government promised the people land in this new area if they left.

Many of the Native people, particularly members of the Cherokee tribe, tried to live peacefully among the white settlers. They joined in the everyday activities of their new communities. They learned English. They even began practicing Christianity. It soon became obvious, though, that staying wasn't an option. What the government really wanted was for the Native Americans to leave.

President Jackson painted a hopeful picture to the Native Americans as he urged them to move westward. "My friends," he told them, "circumstances render it impossible that you can flourish in the midst of a civilized community. You have but one remedy within your reach. And that is to remove to the west, and the sooner you do this, the sooner will commence your career of improvement and prosperity."[3]

Between 1831 and 1839, members of the Cherokee, Chickasaw, Choctaw, Creek, and Seminole tribes traveled west in a migration now known as the Trail of Tears. It was given this name because of the hardships the people faced along the way

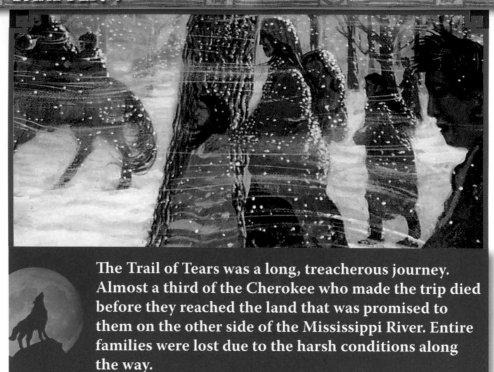

The Trail of Tears was a long, treacherous journey. Almost a third of the Cherokee who made the trip died before they reached the land that was promised to them on the other side of the Mississippi River. Entire families were lost due to the harsh conditions along the way.

to their new land in Oklahoma. Nearly a third of the 15,000 Cherokee who began this forced migration died before they reached their destination.[4]

Most Native Americans who traveled the Trail of Tears took little more than the clothes on their backs. They would be starting over in this new area. Although entire families were lost along the way, the Native people who survived the agonizing voyage made a new life for themselves in their new home.

When gold was discovered in California, it became apparent that the US government wanted to develop land to the west of the Mississippi as well. At first, many Native Americans tried to help the settlers as they headed west. Native people sold some of the game they had hunted to the hungry travelers. Native Americans also worked as guides and messengers between the wagon trains. Still, many white Americans thought of the Indians as savages who would harm them if given the chance.

The government decided to meet with the tribes to help calm the fears of the white people. In 1851, the Treaty of Fort Laramie was signed. Through the agreement, the Indians vowed not to harm the white travelers. They would also allow the government to construct roads and forts through the area. In return, the government agreed to honor the boundaries of the Native people's land and to make annual payments to them in exchange for their use of it.

Once again, however, the government's hunger for land proved to be more important than its word. The Native people who had already been forced west of the Mississippi River would soon be forced onto reservations. These smaller areas of land were established for the Indians in exchange for the additional land the US government was now taking from them.

Many Native Americans who had made new homes along the Mississippi River were forced to move yet again, this time onto reservations.

Reservations still exist across the United States. Making a living on these lands continues to be a difficult task for many Native Americans.

Today, more than 300 reservations still exist in the United States, but making a living on them is challenging for many of the Native people. Poverty is common on reservations. High dropout rates, alcoholism and drug abuse, and violence all add to the problem. These issues help create a cycle where the poorest Native Americans stay poor. On some reservations, the unemployment rate has reached levels as high as 75 percent.

Many Native Americans are rising to the challenge of creating a future for themselves through business. Some Native people are starting their own businesses on the reservations. Others are going to school or opening companies outside the reservations. Both groups are making a huge difference in the world of Native American industry.

GIVING NATIVE AMERICAN COMPANIES A LEG UP

Today the United States government is making efforts to help Native American businesses. A program called Section 8(a) has been created to assist small companies that are owned by minorities. The program awards government sole-source contracts to small businesses like these. The contracts must be for less than $20 million, however, as the program's focus is on helping small companies grow into larger ones.

Former United States Senator Ted Stevens from Alaska took this program a step further when he added a new rule. It made it possible for Alaskan Native American companies to win contracts even larger than $20 million. Many people in other US states aren't thrilled with this arrangement, though. They feel that it gives the Alaskan tribes an unfair advantage over other minority businesses.

Former United States Senator Ted Stevens *(center)* made a big change in the Section 8(a) program. He made it possible for businesses owned by Alaskan Native Americans to win government contracts worth more than $20 million. Sadly, Stevens died in 2010 in a plane crash.

CHAPTER 2

Playing

THE ODDS

Today one of the biggest industries associated with Native Americans is the gaming business. From bingo and slot machines to blackjack and roulette, gambling has become a big business for many tribes across the United States over the last few decades. Nearly 500 casinos can be found on reservations in 28 US states. Together they bring in a total of more than $27 billion each year. These businesses provide more than 628,000 jobs nationwide.[1]

You may wonder how Native Americans got so heavily involved with gaming. After all, their ancestors didn't play games like craps or keno. The simple answer is that gaming has nothing to do with traditional Native American culture. One of the reasons that gaming businesses have flourished on many reservations is that they aren't allowed most other places. Because the reservations aren't governed by the states, Native Americans can offer the public something that other areas cannot. The

Gaming businesses like Gun Lake Casino in Wayland, Michigan, have become very popular on reservations over the last decade or so. Almost 500 of them can be found on various reservations across the United States. Most Indian-owned casinos have been extremely successful, since they aren't allowed in most other places.

gaming industry has enabled many tribes to become more self-sufficient. It didn't happen overnight, though.

The first Native American gaming business opened its doors in 1979. It was run by the Seminole tribe on their reservation in Hollywood, Florida. This high-stakes bingo hall drew immediate disapproval from the state, which tried to shut it down. When the Seminoles refused, the matter became the subject of multiple court battles. By 1981, the dispute had gone all the way to the United States Supreme Court, which ultimately ruled in favor of the tribe and its right to run the business.

The US Supreme Court made another ruling on the matter in 1987 when California tried to stop the Cabazon Band of Mission Indians from running casinos on their reservations there. This time the court's decision was a broader one. It stated that federally-recognized tribes have the right to operate casinos outside the jurisdiction of the states in which they are located. Since reservations are considered sovereign entities, the states could not directly prohibit tribes from running casinos on their land.

Casinos still attract their share of disagreement and controversy. Many people worry that casinos will have a negative effect on nearby communities. University of Georgia economist David B. Mustard and Earl L. Grinols of Baylor University took a close look at crime rates between 1977 and 1996 in US counties with casinos. Their findings indicated that there is a cause for concern in these areas. After the first year, crime began to rise slowly. By the fifth year, the numbers were staggering. Burglaries had gone up 50 percent, auto thefts had increased 78 percent, and aggravated assaults had risen 91 percent. The biggest increase, though, was in robberies—136 percent.[2]

Despite their critics, casinos also have their share of supporters both on and off the reservations. Phil Austin publishes *The Oneida Daily Dispatch* in upstate New York. He thinks that the Turning Stone Resort and Casino has helped to revitalize his local economy since the business opened. "Without it, we'd be in the middle of nowhere and we'd be dead in the water."[3]

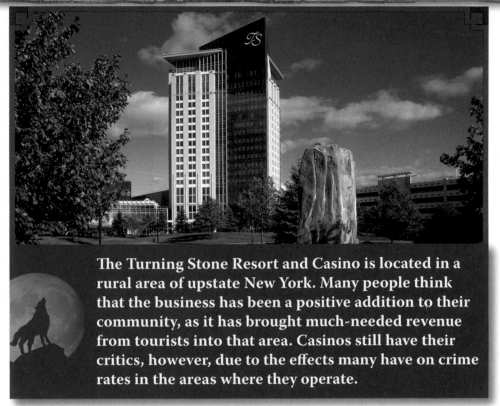

The Turning Stone Resort and Casino is located in a rural area of upstate New York. Many people think that the business has been a positive addition to their community, as it has brought much-needed revenue from tourists into that area. Casinos still have their critics, however, due to the effects many have on crime rates in the areas where they operate.

Joseph W. Jaskiewicz is the mayor of Montville, Connecticut. He says the Mohegan Sun, a casino and resort in Montville, has done wonders for the surrounding communities. The Mohegan tribe signed an agreement with the town to provide it with $500,000 a year from the casino's profits.

States do not have the right to tax casinos on reservations, but many tribes have agreed to share their profits with state governments nonetheless. Arizona, California, Connecticut, Michigan, New Mexico, New York, and Wisconsin all have revenue-sharing agreements in place with the casino-owning tribes in their states. Not only are the tribes now self-sufficient, but they also provide important revenue for the states in which they operate. Michigan uses this money to help fund new businesses, tourism, and arts, for example.

Connecticut has been able to create jobs with their added revenue. The Foxwoods Resort Casino in Mashantucket, Connecticut, has increased traffic in the nearby town of North Stonington significantly. Traffic on Route 2, the main road through the town, has jumped from 8,800 cars each day to 25,000 since the casino opened.[4] This increase was a big change for a town so small that it doesn't even have a police department. Before Foxwoods opened its doors, a single state trooper patrolled North Stonington. Since then, two additional full-time troopers have been hired. The casino has created a greater need for law enforcement, but it has also provided the state with enough money to pay for the new positions.

Jaskiewicz points out that the Mohegan Sun brings money to his state in other ways as well. Tourists may come to Montville for the casino, but they also end up spending money at other businesses during their stay. "We used to be a drive-through town," he explained. "We're no longer a drive-through town. People have a reason to stop."[5]

Mohegan Sun in Montville, Connecticut, is a modern facility that incorporates traditional Native American culture. The business offers a colorful backdrop inspired by Native American art. Visitors can spend time gaming, shopping, or enjoying live entertainment during their stay.

The town of Montville reaps many rewards from the Mohegan Sun. The casino shares more than $500,000 with the town each year. The town's other restaurants and shops also pick up business from the people who come to the area to visit the casino.

Sharing profits with the states has proven to be a smart move for many tribes. In Florida, for instance, the Seminoles offered to pay the state $1 billion over five years in exchange for exclusive rights to certain games. Under the agreement, the tribe operates the only blackjack tables in the state. John Fontana is the president of the Seminole Hard Rock Hotel and Casino in Tampa. When asked about the connection between the casino's success and its lack of competition, he says, "It doesn't hurt to be in the market by ourselves, I'll tell you that."[6]

The Seminoles have done so well in this business that they have expanded it beyond the borders of their reservations. In 2007, the tribe used some of the money that it had made to buy the entire Hard Rock International franchise. This company owns

The Seminole Hard Rock Hotel and Casino is just one of many Hard Rock businesses located all over the world.

casinos, hotels, and restaurants in fifty-five countries around the world.

For the Seminoles, the casino business venture has been an enormous success. As Fontana shared, "We've gone from 95 percent of our support coming from federal and state grants to now being completely economically self-sufficient, and even giving money back to the state. And our money is kept here in the state, and is a huge economic driver for the state of Florida."[7]

SUCCEEDING
IN HARD TIMES

Despite the economic problems the rest of the country has faced in recent years, the Native American gaming industry appears to be booming. In 2011, tribes in Florida earned a total of $2.16 billion from gaming, an increase of 5 percent from the previous year. The 2011 revenues of California's tribes only grew by about 2 percent from 2010, but they still brought in more money overall than any other state's tribes: $6.9 billion. This number represents about a quarter of the total revenue from Native American gaming nationwide.[8]

Opening any business can be a big gamble, but the risk has paid off for many tribes that now operate casinos.

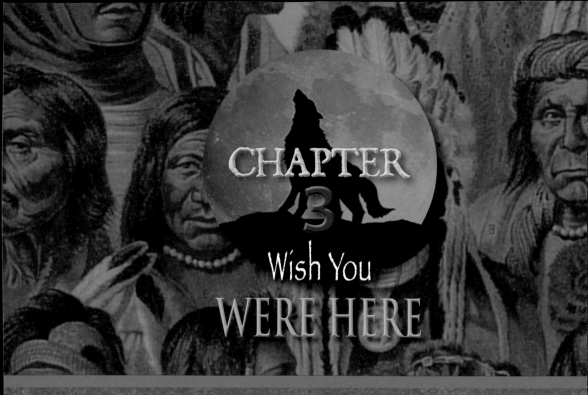

CHAPTER 3

Wish You WERE HERE

Casinos aren't the only attractions that draw visitors to Indian reservations. Native American traditions like powwows have fascinated other Americans, as well as people from other countries, for many years. This fascination has created an important opportunity for many tribes in the way of tourism. Visiting an Indian reservation offers tourists a chance to experience the tribe's culture firsthand.

Of course, not all Native Americans welcome visitors. Some tribes prefer to keep their land and their customs more private. Ben Sherman is the president of the Native Tourism Alliance in Louisville, Colorado. He explains, "Many tribes have some amount of skepticism—and for good reason. They have had their cultures and their lands exploited in the past by outsiders, by people who are not tribal members and who perhaps benefited from some manner of tourism."[1]

One group that has plenty of reason to feel tourist-shy is the Quileute tribe in the state of Washington. Stephenie Meyer's

Both Native and non-Native Americans are drawn to traditional events such as powwows. Many tribes welcome visitors interested in attending these elaborate celebrations of Native American culture. Music, dancing, and colorful costumes are just a few of the things guests will see and hear at this type of event.

wildly popular *Twilight* book and movie series has brought a great deal of attention to the tribe and its reservation in La Push in recent years. The series is set in the nearby town of Forks, and many of the characters are Quileute werewolves, the natural enemies of the town's vampire family. Meyers based these characters on the real tribe's spiritual connection to wolves. The first Quileute people are indeed said to have been transformed from wolves into humans. But how do the Quileute feel about their tribal story being exaggerated into a supernatural teen phenomenon? And how do they feel about the spotlight that Meyer has cast on them?

Many Quileute members have responded to the interest from fans of the series quite well. Most fans understand that *Twilight* is fiction. These individuals come to La Push to learn about the

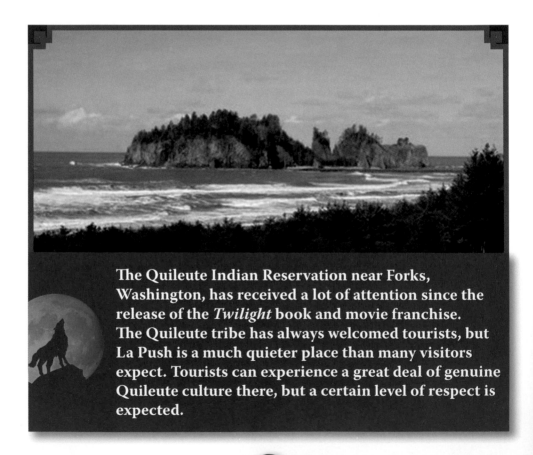

The Quileute Indian Reservation near Forks, Washington, has received a lot of attention since the release of the *Twilight* book and movie franchise. The Quileute tribe has always welcomed tourists, but La Push is a much quieter place than many visitors expect. Tourists can experience a great deal of genuine Quileute culture there, but a certain level of respect is expected.

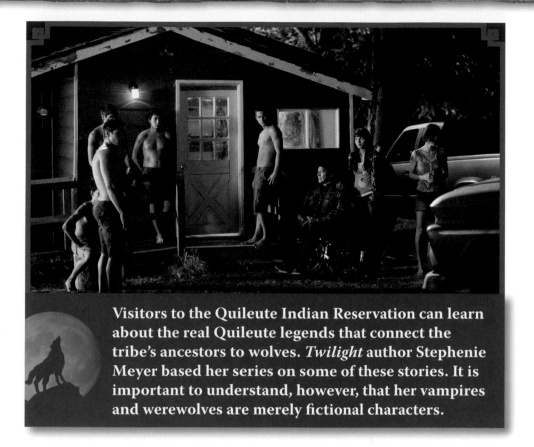

Visitors to the Quileute Indian Reservation can learn about the real Quileute legends that connect the tribe's ancestors to wolves. *Twilight* author Stephenie Meyer based her series on some of these stories. It is important to understand, however, that her vampires and werewolves are merely fictional characters.

real Quileute tribe, and many tribe members welcome them. As Tribal Council Chairman Tony Foster points out, "The Quileute have always been a welcoming tribe."[2]

Certainly *Twilight* has created an opportunity for the Quileute to turn this attention into tourism dollars. While making a living is important, though, the tribe also wants to maintain a certain level of privacy and respect. They have been fortunate enough to find a happy medium. For instance, they have allowed outsiders to witness the Wolf Dance, a meaningful part of the tribe's weekly drum and healing circle. They do not permit visitors to take photographs of the ritual, however.

The *Twilight* series has also brought tourists to the Quileute Oceanside Resort. This attraction includes thirty-three cabins, twenty-eight motel rooms, and a campground and RV park. A

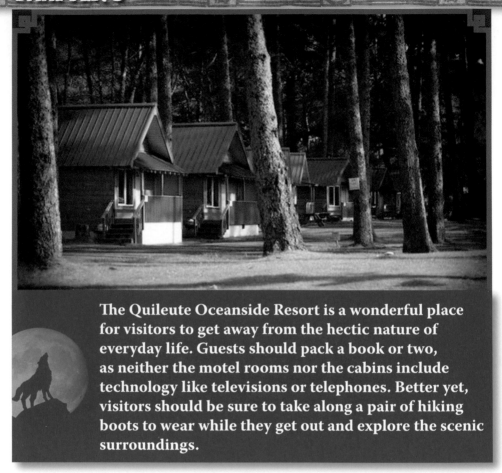

The Quileute Oceanside Resort is a wonderful place for visitors to get away from the hectic nature of everyday life. Guests should pack a book or two, as neither the motel rooms nor the cabins include technology like televisions or telephones. Better yet, visitors should be sure to take along a pair of hiking boots to wear while they get out and explore the scenic surroundings.

stay at this resort isn't like a vacation at many other vacation spots. Neither the cabins nor the motel rooms include televisions or phones for the guests. The atmosphere is designed to give its guests a sense of separation from the rest of the world.

If a quiet, restful vacation isn't your thing, you can almost certainly find another reservation that matches your interests. Whether you enjoy natural history or contemporary art and culture, you are sure to find it on one of the many Indian reservations around the United States. The Museum of the Cherokee Indian in North Carolina shares the tribe's 11,000-year history with tourists. The Big Cypress Seminole Indian Reservation in Florida is home to an extensive Native American art collection.

The Museum of the Cherokee Indian is filled with artifacts and reproductions which tell the extensive history of the tribe.

The Navajo Nation offers its visitors day-long hikes to its Betatakin and Keet Seel ruins. Some tribes have even recreated Indian villages that tourists can walk through to get a better sense of the daily lives of tribe members long ago.

Many tribes would welcome tourists, but because of widespread poverty, creating tourist attractions in these places can be extremely difficult. Some people assume that issues like alcoholism and high school dropout rates are the reasons for the vicious cycle of poverty on many reservations. Other people point to the way the land is owned as the problem.

A great deal of the land on the reservations is held communally. This means that the land technically belongs to everyone. Individuals on reservations often have a harder time getting credit, because they cannot use their land as collateral. Families are also less likely to build permanent homes on land that they don't own.

Manny Jules is a former chief of the Kamloops Indian band in British Columbia, Canada. Land is held communally there, as well. As he explained, "When you don't have individual property rights, you can't build, you can't be bonded, you can't pass on wealth. A lot of small businesses never get started, because

In 1969 Native American chiefs in Canada united to form the Union of British Columbia Indian Chiefs (UBCIC). The organization, which still exists today, was founded on the principle that despite individual or tribal differences, Native American people are stronger when they work together.

people can't leverage property [to raise funds]. This act would free our entrepreneurial spirit, but it's going to take a freeing of our imagination. We have to become part of the national and global economies."[3]

Another problem standing in the way of business on the reservations is the fact that contracts between Native Americans living on the reservations and businesses outside the reservations cannot always be enforced. If a person living on the reservation refuses to make loan payments to a bank, for instance, the bank cannot do much about it. Judgments from American courts cannot be enforced on the reservations. Banks and other businesses must take their disputes to the tribal courts instead.

Bill Yellowtail is a former Crow official. He is also a former Montana state senator. He shares, "We're a long way from having a reliable business climate. Businesses coming to the reservation ask, 'What am I getting into?' The tribal courts are not reliable dispute forums."[4]

FINDING BALANCE

Even though tribe members need to make money, not all Native Americans want to put their cultures on display for tourists. Leslie Kedelty is the executive director of the American Indian Alaska Native Tourism Association in Albuquerque, New Mexico. She states, "When we talk to tribes across the United States about travel and tourism, we really want them to understand that they don't have to share everything with the visitor. We as Indian people have traditional knowledge that we can keep to ourselves. We don't have to publicize those sacred sites that are very important to us."[5]

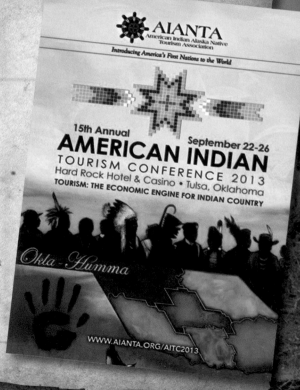

Each year the American Indian Alaska Native Tourism Association (AIANTA) holds a conference. The event offers Native businesses an opportunity to share knowledge and experience in the field of tourism. Business owners can attend workshops and presentations to help them grow their companies.

CHAPTER 4

Doing Business—On and Off—
THE RESERVATIONS

Just as not all Native Americans live on reservations, not all Native American businesses are located on reservations either. Ron Colombe is a member of the Lakota tribe. He was born on the Rosebud Reservation in South Dakota, but he now resides in Aiken, South Carolina, where he and his wife own a store called Elk Eagle Originals. The business sells only authentic Native American items such as framed artwork, jewelry, pottery, and hand-woven rugs made by tribes from all over the country.

Colombe is also a craftsman himself. He makes jewelry, candles, sandstone oil lamps, and unique framed images using bird feathers and leather. In addition to being an artist, Colombe is a prose poet as well. His love of words is evident in the many conversations he has with his customers. "I'm always eager to talk," Colombe shares. "It's a passion of mine for people to learn about Native American things, because there are people out there who think Native Americans don't exist anymore, that we're a people of the past."[1]

Ron Colombe is a Native American business owner in Aiken, South Carolina, who sells authentic Native American items. He is also a poet and a craftsman himself. One of his favorite pastimes is educating his customers about modern Native American culture.

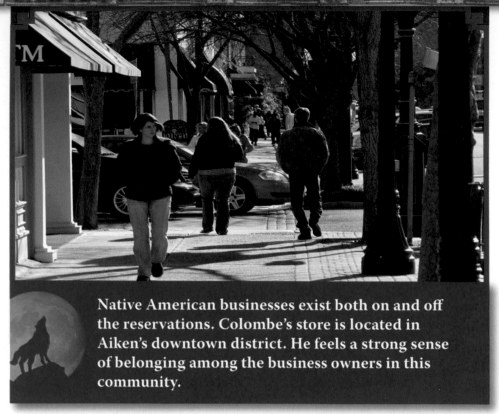

Native American businesses exist both on and off the reservations. Colombe's store is located in Aiken's downtown district. He feels a strong sense of belonging among the business owners in this community.

Colombe's business is part of both Native American industry and the local Aiken economy. He feels a true sense of belonging in both worlds. "This is the place to be if you're a small business owner," he said of his store's location. "The downtown area is very nice. It seems like people look out for each other in the business community."[2]

Native Americans in Oklahoma have a tremendous business resource at their disposal. It's called the Native American Business Enterprise Center (NABEC), and its purpose is to help Native American businesspeople get the financing they need to open and grow their companies. In its first three years, the center helped Native American businesses access almost $75 million in loans and other forms of financial assistance. NABEC also helps with business plans, career development, and even drawing up contracts. More than 360 jobs have been created as a result of these efforts.[3]

**Contech, LLC has constructed many buildings in and around
Broken Arrow, Oklahoma.**

One of the center's biggest success stories is Contech, LLC,
an earthwork and commercial concrete construction company in
the city of Broken Arrow. With the help of NABEC, Contech has
increased its revenue by 200 percent and increased its workforce
from forty people to one hundred.[4] The company has built a
warehouse more than 1 million square feet in area and a four-
story parking garage. It serves many clients, including educational
institutions and the government.

For twenty-three years, Tom Seth Smith was the president
and chief executive of Rural Enterprises of Oklahoma, the
company that created the NABEC. He reports that working with
the government is proving to be a positive move for many Native
American companies. "More and more tribes are getting involved
in federal contracting, and by extension we're seeing more
individuals working with the tribes."[5]

Native American businesses seem to be growing in numerous ways. Not only are new businesses popping up, but companies already in business are expanding. The Angel of the Winds Casino is located on the Stillaguamish reservation just outside Arlington, Washington. In 2011, though, the tribe decided to open a new type of business: a gas station. Travis O'Neil is the general manager of the casino. He sees the gas station as another way the business can offer hospitality to its guests. On the day the tribe broke ground on the project, he shared, "With the price of fuel being top of mind for everyone, we will offer a competitively priced product and add another amenity to our property."[6]

Koran Andrews is the chief executive officer of STECO, the company that owns both the casino and the gas station. He was also very proud of this addition to the tribe's businesses. "I don't think my grandparents anticipated that we would have come so

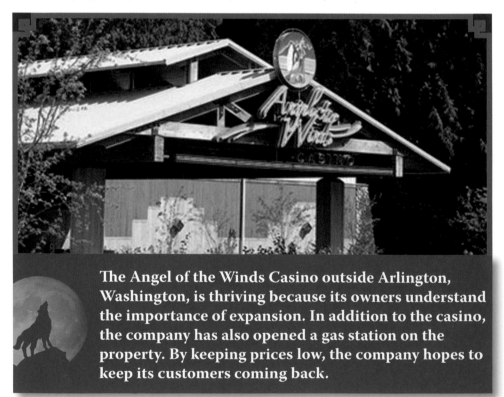

The Angel of the Winds Casino outside Arlington, Washington, is thriving because its owners understand the importance of expansion. In addition to the casino, the company has also opened a gas station on the property. By keeping prices low, the company hopes to keep its customers coming back.

In an effort to use recyclable goods at his casino, Koran Andrews discovered another huge business opportunity.

far. I'm so excited to have been part of the team that's accomplished this. It's an expression of our sovereignty as a tribe, but it also allows us to serve the community."[7]

The gas station wasn't the end of the Stillaguamish expansion into new areas of business. Andrews wanted to begin using recyclable cups in his tribe's casino, and so he took a tour of a plastics factory that offered these cups. He was so impressed with MicroGREEN Polymers, Inc. that in 2013 he ended up investing $5 million in the company.

"After the tour, it became very clear to me that this is a brand new technology that can really do some good. Not just for our local economy, but for the environment as well," Andrews explained. "It was kind of meant to be. They fall in line with what we value in regards to doing what we can for this planet while we're here. And that's really important to Indian tribes— protecting Mother Earth."[8]

Native American values center around a deep respect for Mother Earth. Investing in companies that make recyclable products offer tribes the chance to succeed in business while promoting causes which are important to them.

Andrews is hoping to get other Native American tribes to invest in the company as well. As he points out, the product offers both environmental and economic advantages. The cups use 50 percent less plastic and weigh between 50 and 80 percent less than average cups. Andrews adds, "MicroGREEN's cups are generally able to be sold for a more competitive price than your average plastic cup. There is definitely an economic benefit."[9]

STRIKING OIL

Native American tribes in North and South Dakota and Montana could be on the verge of a huge economic boost in the form of oil—possibly as many as 24 billion barrels' worth. An amount like this could lessen America's dependence on foreign oil, and make the tribes very wealthy in the process. John Jurrius is the chief executive and founder of Native American Resource Partners (NARP). This organization works with tribal nations to establish joint energy companies. Both NARP and tribes in these three states are currently waiting to see if there is indeed oil deep in the land.

Jurrius notes that other tribes who have started energy companies with NARP have had great success. The Southern Ute tribe in southwest Colorado, for example, has experienced many changes as a result of their partnership with NARP. "The dropout rate in schools there was 50 percent, now it is 10 percent," he shares. "They have 135 kids in college each year—compared to none before. They have their own retirement programs and healthcare budget. The Nation even achieved a triple-A rating to [sell] bonds to build a hospital for the community."[10]

Oil drill

CHAPTER 5

The Road to
THE FUTURE

The future of Native American industry lies within the youth of the hundreds of tribes across the United States. Many of these young people can look to other Native Americans who have achieved success in business. A great example is Dave Anderson, better known by the name of his popular restaurant chain— Famous Dave's of America. Born in Chicago to Ojibwe and Choctaw parents, Anderson opened his first location in 1994. Since then, he has turned the small company into a nationwide business of about 200 restaurants.

Anderson's life hasn't always been an easy one. He grew up on and off Indian reservations. He graduated from high school in the bottom half of his class. In adulthood, he had numerous business failures. He also struggled with alcoholism.

While he was in treatment for his alcohol addiction, Anderson finally decided to turn his life around. The first thing he did was earn his master's degree in public administration from Harvard University. He then put his knowledge to use by helping other

Restaurant chain owner Dave Anderson overcame many obstacles to become the success he is today. Despite many failures, he managed to create a company with about 200 locations. Today Anderson visits schools to speak to students about how he did it.

Native Americans achieve success in business before he started his own company.

He still wasn't done helping other Native Americans, though. In 2002, Anderson founded the LifeSkills Center for Leadership. The goal of this nonprofit organization is to help teach leadership skills and offer scholarships to Native American and multicultural youth, so they can achieve their dreams too. "It doesn't matter what you come from, what you've been through, you've got to follow your dreams," Anderson has said.[1]

Some Native Americans have achieved their dreams by creating businesses that improve the lives of other Native Americans. One such company is Ho-Chunk, Inc. of Nebraska. This economic development firm employs more than 1,400 people, many of whom are Winnebago tribe members. It operates many different types of businesses including car sales, construction, advertising, and finance firms. One of the company's goals is to create jobs and employ as many tribe members as it can. Ho-Chunk also runs various nonprofit organizations like the Ho-Chunk Community Development Corporation, which offers economic, educational, and housing programs for people living on the Winnebago Indian Reservation.

Lance Morgan (right) is the CEO of Ho-Chunk. One of the biggest goals of his company is to help other Native Americans find success in the business world.

Native American industry in the twenty-first century has come to mean many things. And it is bound to expand even further in the next several decades as more young Native Americans pursue higher education. Some of them are earning degrees with the help of other American businesses—like the AT&T-Western Governors University (WGU) Native American Scholarship Program. The AT&T Foundation got involved in the program in 2010 when it made a $150,000 donation to set up the first thirty scholarships for Native American tribe members, their spouses, and people living and working in Native American communities.

Students from fourteen US states have already used the scholarships for nineteen different degree programs. They are working towards either bachelor's or master's degrees in one of four different fields: business, education, health, and information technology. In all, WGU offers more than fifty different online programs for bachelor's, master's, and post-baccalaureate degrees.

James Linderman is a Chickasaw Nation member from Cushing, Oklahoma, who is working towards a BS in IT Security. He doesn't plan to stop there, though. "I would like to develop a complete software package that will teach the language of my people to my people. At the same time I would like to incorporate lessons in the history and culture of the Chickasaw people so that Chickasaws know what it is to be Chickasaw."[2]

Michael Floyd lives in Tracyton, Washington, but he is a member of the Sun'aq Native Alaskan tribe of Kodiak. He is earning a BS in Business Management and feels strongly that Native Americans should not have to limit their careers to running casinos or selling items that are not legal off the reservations. "Native Americans/Alaskans should not have to supply other people's vices to provide for their people." After he earns his degree, Floyd would like to open an inn in Kodiak, Alaska. "The lands are beautiful, and people should see them and enjoy them. I will employ and train Native Alaskans so that

Many Native Americans still make their living by farming.

they can work at home or, if they choose to leave, will have marketable skills."[3]

Not all Native American businesses with promising futures are new ones. Some, like the farms run by the Ak-Chin, Gila River, and Fort McDowell Native Americans in Arizona, have been around for decades. Leona Kakar has headed Ak-Chin's farm board since 1965. She points out, "The farm has been in operation since 1961 . . . We're still going strong." Part of the reason may be the tribe's deep respect for the land. Kakar explains that the farmers nurture it. "As long as we take care of the soil, it will take care of us."[4]

When it comes to farming, the lack of commercial development on tribal lands has proven to be a good thing. Julie Murphee is the director of communications for the Arizona Farm Bureau. She says, "Agriculture on tribal lands is a valuable part of Arizona's $9.2 billion industry. Where development on other land in the state is encroaching on good farmland, tribal lands have the potential to become a growing and significant part of the entire production mix in this industry."[5]

As Native American farmers look to the future, they know that their businesses will have to change with the times. Some are already keeping up quite well. Orlando Moreno is the chief executive of Fort McDowell Yavapai Nation Enterprises. This business already has a water-saving irrigation system. "Any time you can do something more efficiently and conserve a limited resource, it is a worthwhile endeavor," Moreno shares. "Our state-of-the-art irrigation system does just that, and we are very proud and pleased with the results of our investment. I see the next generation of irrigation systems taking advantage of the advances in mobile-networking technology, and as these advances become available and affordable we will explore utilizing them to a greater extent than what we are currently doing."[6]

KEEPING IT TOGETHER

George Rivera is the governor of the Pueblo Pojoaque people of New Mexico. He sees business not only as a necessary source of income, but also as a way of keeping his tribe connected to each other. He doesn't want the Pojoaque to be forced to leave their home to find work. The Hilton Santa Fe Golf Resort & Spa at Buffalo Thunder is a perfect example of the type of business that Rivera thinks will keep the Pojoaque people working close to home. The resort-casino was designed with both the scenic surroundings and Pueblo history in mind. The hotel has nearly 400 rooms, but unlike most resorts this size, it is only five stories high. Rivera says, "The concept was to take the most powerful element of nature and have that become part of the theme of the resort."

Rivera is very proud of the project. "It gives the Pueblo Pojoaque identity, and I believe that it will help move in the direction of education and business and preserving the culture and the community as a whole. I think that with the opportunities Buffalo Thunder has it will keep the tribe united into the future."[7]

The Hilton Santa Fe Golf Resort and Spa in New Mexico is unlike any other resort its size. As large as it is, the structure fits perfectly into the natural surroundings of the area. Its design also reflects the history of the Pueblo people.

Chapter 1

1. Laurie Winslow, *Tulsa World,* "Cherokee Data Solutions, Its Owner Win Small-Business Awards," November 10, 2010.
2. Ibid.
3. PBS, *New Perspectives on the West,* "Trail of Tears."
4. PBS, *Africans in America,* "The Trail of Tears."

Chapter 2

1. 500 Nations, "Casinos."
2. Richard Morin, *The Washington Post,* "Casinos and Crime: The Luck Runs Out," May 11, 2006.
3. Bart Jones, *Newsday,* "Communities Report Mixed Experiences With Indian Casinos," June 2, 2009.
4. Ibid.
5. Ibid.
6. Nick Sortal, *SunSentinel,* "Revenues at Indian Casinos Up 5 Percent, According to Report," February 27, 2013.
7. Ibid.
8. Tracy X. Miguel, *Naples Daily News,* "Study: American Indian Casinos, Such as Immokalee's Showing Yearly Growth," March 12, 2013.

Chapter 3

1. Bryn Nelson, *High Country News,* "Threatened by a Tsunami of Tourism, A Tribe Opens Up," June 25, 2012.
2. Ibid.
3. John Koppisch, *Forbes,* "Why Are Indian Reservations So Poor? A Look At The Bottom 1%," December 13, 2011.
4. Ibid.
5. Bryn Nelson, *High Country News,* "Threatened by a Tsunami of Tourism, A Tribe Opens Up," June 25, 2012.

Chapter 4

1. Amy Banton, *Aiken Standard,* "Native American Store Joins Downtown's Business Family," July 13, 2012.

2. Ibid.
3. Brian Brus, *The Journal Record,* "Bearing Fruit: Rural Enterprises of Oklahoma Center Supports Native American Businesses," December 20, 2010.
4. Ibid.
5. Ibid.
6. Kirk Boxleitner, *The Arlington Times,* "Stillaguamish Tribe Breaks Ground on New Gas Station," July 13, 2011.
7. Ibid.
8. Jenny Kalish, *Waste & Recyling News,* "Native American Tribe Invests in Sustainable Plastic Company," vol. 18, February 4, 2013.
9. Ibid.
10. Helen Avery, *Euromoney,* "Oil Boom Brightens Native Americans' Prospects," vol. 41, October 2011, p. 20.

Chapter 5

1. Susanne Nadeau, *Grand Forks Herald,* "Mahnomen, Minn.: Three Nations," November 30, 2006.
2. PR Newswire, "31 Scholarships Awarded to Help Native Americans Attend Online University," March 27, 2012.
3. Ibid.
4. Debra Utacia Krol, *Arizona Capital Times,* "Growth Industry: Native American Farms in Arizona Reclaim Heritage, Expand Operations," August 7, 2009.
5. Ibid.
6. Ibid.
7. Carlo Wolff, *Lodging Hospitality,* "Going Native," vol. 65, February 2009, p. 21.

*Full bibliographic information including web addresses can be found in Works Consulted

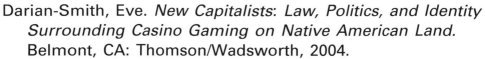

Darian-Smith, Eve. *New Capitalists*: *Law, Politics, and Identity Surrounding Casino Gaming on Native American Land.* Belmont, CA: Thomson/Wadsworth, 2004.

Lawlor, Mary. *Public Native America*: *Tribal Self-Representation in Museums, Powwows, and Casinos.* Piscataway, NJ: Rutgers University Press, 2006.

Miller, Robert J. *Reservation " Capitalism".* Santa Barbara, CA: Praeger, 2012.

On the Internet

Famous Dave Anderson
   http://www.famousdaveanderson.com/

Michigan State University: Native American Business Institute
   http://mbp.broad.msu.edu/nabi/

The National Center for American Indian Enterprise Development
   http://www.ncaied.org/

Quileute Nation
   http://www.quileutenation.org/

The Seminole Tribe of Florida
   http://www.semtribe.com/

500 Nations. "Casinos." http://500nations.com/Indian_Casinos. asp

Avery, Helen. "Oil Boom Brightens Native Americans' Prospects." *Euromoney,* vol. 41, October 2011, p. 20.

Banton, Amy. "Native American Store Joins Downtown's Business Family." *Aiken Standard,* July 13, 2012.

Boxleitner, Kirk. "Stillaguamish Tribe Breaks Ground on New Gas Station." *The Arlington Times,* July 13, 2011.

Brus, Brian. "Bearing Fruit: Rural Enterprises of Oklahoma Center Supports Native American Businesses." *The Journal Record,* December 20, 2010.

Jones, Bart. "Communities Report Mixed Experiences With Indian Casinos." *Newsday,* June 2, 2009.

Kalish, Jenny. "Native American Tribe Invests in Sustainable Plastic Company." *Waste & Recyling News,* vol. 18, February 4, 2013.

Koppisch, John. "Why Are Indian Reservations So Poor? A Look At The Bottom 1%." *Forbes,* December 13, 2011. http://www.forbes.com/sites/johnkoppisch/2011/12/13/ why-are-indian-reservations-so-poor-a-look-at-the-bottom-1/

Krol, Debra Utacia. "Growth Industry: Native American Farms in Arizona Reclaim Heritage, Expand Operations." *Arizona Capital Times,* August 7, 2009.

LifeSkills Center for Leadership. "LifeSkills Foundation Founder, 'Famous Dave' Anderson." http://www.lifeskills-center.org/

Miguel, Tracy X. "Study: American Indian Casinos, Such as Immokalee's Showing Yearly Growth." *Naples Daily News,* March 12, 2013. http://www.naplesnews.com/ news/2013/mar/12/ study-american-indian-casinos-such-as-immokalees/

Morin, Richard. "Casinos and Crime: The Luck Runs Out." *The Washington Post,* May 11, 2006.

Nadeau, Susanne. "Mahnomen, Minn.: Three Nations." *Grand Forks Herald,* November 30, 2006.

National Conference of State Legislatures (NCSL). "State Casino Taxes." http://www.ncsl.org/issues-research/econ/state-casino-taxes.aspx

Nelson, Bryn. "Threatened by a Tsunami of Tourism, A Tribe Opens Up." *High Country News,* June 25, 2012.

PBS. "The Trail of Tears." *Africans in America.* http://www.pbs.org/wgbh/aia/part4/4h1567.html

PBS. "Trail of Tears." *New Perspectives on the West.* http://www.pbs.org/weta/thewest/program/episodes/two/trailtears.htm

Potter, Matthew. "Federal Government Continues Moves to Restrict Native American Contracts and Companies." *Defense Procurement News,* June 14, 2010. http://www.defenseprocurementnews.com/2010/06/14/federal-government-continues-moves-to-restrict-native-american-contracts-and-companies/#ixzz0qpwKfwcb

PR Newswire. "31 Scholarships Awarded to Help Native Americans Attend Online University." March 27, 2012.

Sharpe, Kimberly. "Tourist-Friendly Indian Reservations in the US." *USA Today.* http://traveltips.usatoday.com/touristfriendly-indian-reservations-103336.html

Sortal, Nick. "Revenues at Indian Casinos Up 5 Percent, According to Report." *SunSentinel,* February 27, 2013.

Winslow, Laurie. "Cherokee Data Solutions, Its Owner Win Small-Business Awards." *Tulsa World,* November 10, 2010. http://www.tulsaworld.com/business/article.aspx?subjectid=46&articleid=20101110_46_E1_CUTLIN156003

Wolff, Carlo. "Going Native." *Lodging Hospitality,* vol. 65, February 2009.

alcoholism (AL-kuh-haw-liz-uhm): an addiction to or dependence on alcoholic beverages

bonded (BON-did): insured against losses from dishonest behavior

collateral (kuh-LAT-er-uhl): property pledged to secure the payment of a loan

franchise (FRAN-chahyz): a business operating under a license to use another company's brand name and products or services

hospitality (hos-pi-TAL-i-tee): part of the tourism industry that includes food, lodging, and entertainment

jurisdiction (joor-is-DIK-shuhn): the area over which a government or other entity has authority to govern

marketable (MAHR-ki-tuh-buhl): able to be sold

powwow (POU-wou): a Native American ceremony involving food, music, and dancing

reservation (rez-er-VEY-shuhn): a piece of land set apart for use by a particular group, such as an Indian tribe

revenue (REV-uh-noo): money coming in

savage (SAV-ij): an uncivilized or barbaric person

self-sufficient (self-suh-FISH-uhnt): able to provide for one's own needs without outside assistance

subcontractor (suhb-KON-trak-ter): a person or business hired to do part of another's work